Animal Lives

BATS

Sally Morgan

QEB Publishing

Copyright © QEB Publishing, Inc. 2008

Published in the United States by
QEB Publishing, Inc.
23062 La Cadena Drive
Laguna Hills, CA 92653

www.qeb-publishing.com

Library of Congress Control Number: 2008011523

ISBN 978 1 59566 535 5

Written by Sally Morgan
Design and editorial by East River Partnership

Publisher Steve Evans
Creative Director Zeta Davies

Printed and bound in the United States

Picture Credits

Key: t = top, b = bottom, l = left, r = right,
c = center, FC = front cover

Corbis /Wolfgang Kaehler 8–9, /Christophe
Loviny 27tr; **Ecoscene** /Nicholas & Sherry
Lu Aldridge 29t; **FLPA** /Hugo Willcox/Foto
Natura 4–5, /Krystyna Szulecka 5tr; **Getty**
/Arte Wolfe 4bl, /Michael Durham 14–15,
/Michael & Patricia Fogden 20–21, 24,
/Konrad Wothe 25; **Photolibrary** /Miller
Larry 7t, /Mary Plage 6–7, 14b, /Les Stocker
13, /Richard La Val 18, /Oxford Scientific 19,
/Alastair Shay 28–29; **Photoshot/NHPA**
/Melvin Grey 11tl, 12, 30r, 30c, /Stephen
Dalton 16–17, 22–23, 23tr, 30l /Daniel
Heuclin 20bl; **Shutterstock** /Susan Flashman
1, /Styve Reineck background 2–3, 12–13,
18–19, 24–25, 30–31, 32, /Grigory Kubatyan
10–11, /Graeme Knox 26–27.

Words in **bold** are explained
in the glossary on page 31.

Contents

Bats

Bats are small creatures that rest and sleep during the day and come out at night to feed. Most bats have furry bodies and a pair of leathery wings with which they can fly silently through the air.

Trees and caves

Bats hang upside-down from trees and the walls of caves rather than coming to rest on the ground. They have an unusual ability to 'see with sound' called **echolocation**. Bats use echolocation to find their way around in the dark when hunting.

The flying fox is a fruit bat with a face that looks similar to a fox.

The Bismarck flying fox is a large bat found in Indonesia and Papua New Guinea.

Closest relatives

Bats are **mammals**. Female mammals give birth to live young and feed them milk. Like most other mammals, including rabbits, dogs, and horses, bats have hair covering their body. Bats are most closely related to shrews, moles, and hedgehogs.

Bats, along with insects and birds, are the only animals that can fly.

Bat types

There are about 1,100 species of bat. There are so many, in fact, that one in every five types of mammal is a bat.

Big and small bats

Bats are divided into two groups called the **Megachiroptera** and **Microchiroptera**, or megabats and microbats. Megabats are the fruit bats, which are also known as 'flying foxes.' These are large bats with big, round eyes. Microbats are mostly smaller, insect-eating bats with small eyes and large ears. The smallest microbats, such as the bumblebee bat, have a wingspan of just 2 inches and weigh about 2 grams—the same as a matchstick.

Bat fact!
For a long time, people mistakenly thought that bats were flying mice.

All colors

Although most bats have silky, brown fur, some have white, red, yellow, or black fur. A few types of bat have no fur at all! There are even bats with pink wings and pink ears.

The fur of this female red bat ends with a white tip that looks like frost.

These tiny Honduran white bats have fluffy, white fur, yellow noses and ears, and black wings.

Where do you find bats?

Many different types of **habitat** provide homes for bats. Microbats are found in most parts of the world, except the very cold Arctic and Antarctic. The larger megabats only live in hot places.

Bat habitats

Large fruit bats live in **tropical** rain forests where they eat fruit from the many fruit trees that grow there. Microbats, on the other hand, are found in forests, deserts, and grasslands all around the world.

These fruit bats are sheltering under a roof.

Bat fact!

Bats that **roost** under the roofs of buildings are often protected by law and must not be disturbed.

8

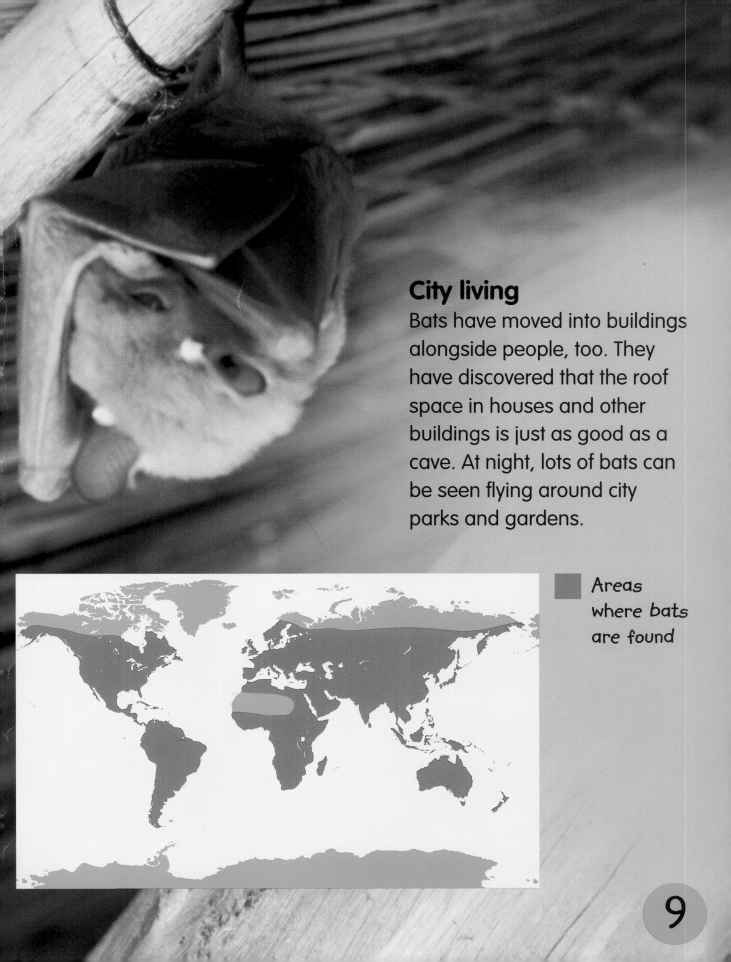

City living

Bats have moved into buildings alongside people, too. They have discovered that the roof space in houses and other buildings is just as good as a cave. At night, lots of bats can be seen flying around city parks and gardens.

Areas where bats are found

Bat caves and roosts

When bats are not flying, they are roosting. A bat's roost is a dry place where it is safe from **predators**. Bat roosts can be found in roof spaces, under bridges, in dark caves, in the branches and hollows of trees, and even under fallen logs.

Bat colonies

Most bats live and roost together in a group called a colony. As many as 200,000 fruit bats may roost in one tree, while millions of bats can roost in the same cave.

Bats prefer to roos in caves that are neither too hot nor too cold.

This brown long-eared bat is using its front and back claws to cling to a roof.

Weak legs

Unlike birds, bats cannot stand on the ground. This is because they have very weak legs. Instead, bats hang upside-down, gripping with their sharp claws. They have special **tendons** in their legs that keep their toes curled and stop them from letting go when they fall asleep.

Crawling around

A bat's knees face backward. This helps it to crawl four-legged across a cave ceiling, much like a spider. Special claws on its wings and legs allow it to hold on tightly.

Bat fact!

During the 1960s, more than 50 million Mexican free-tailed bats lived in one cave. Today, the largest roost contains 20 million bats.

Beginning life

The pipistrelle is a tiny microbat that weighs just 4 grams. Its life cycle starts when the male and female come together and mate. The female is **pregnant** for about three months before giving birth to a baby bat. This baby is called a 'pup.' When she gives birth, the female hangs from her thumbs and holds her wings under her body so that she can catch her pup as it is born!

Bat fact!

The female hammer-headed bat chooses her mate by flying along a row of about 100 males lined up along branches and flapping their wings to attract her attention.

Blind pup

When it is born, the pup weighs about one-quarter of its mother's weight. It is blind and completely helpless, depending on its mother for warmth and food. To survive, the tiny pup has to cling tightly to its mother's fur and feed on her milk.

A tiny pipistrelle pup snuggles up to its mother to feed and keep warm.

Growing up

The young pipistrelle bat feeds on its mother's milk for about six weeks. By the time it is three weeks old, however, it has already grown teeth and can feed on insects as well. The young pup develops very quickly in the first weeks of its life, and is fully grown by the time it is only two months old.

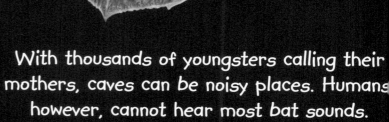

With thousands of youngsters calling their mothers, caves can be noisy places. Humans however, cannot hear most bat sounds.

When young, pipistrelle bats have to learn which insects are good to eat.

Hunting for food

To feed her pup and herself, the pipistrelle mother has to go out hunting for food several times a night. While out hunting, she leaves her pup in a **creche** with other young bats to be looked after by another female. When the mother returns, she can recognize her own pup from its high-pitched squeak.

Catching insects

The pup can start to fly when it is about three weeks old. At first, the mother helps her pup to find food. But it is not long before the young bat can catch insects on its own.

Bat fact!

A female vampire bat will adopt an orphan pup that has lost its own mother.

Bat food

Bats have to eat a lot of food every day to keep their body working properly. If a bat goes without food for even just two days, it may die.

Frogs, rats and mice

Although most of the smaller microbats eat insects, some also feed on frogs, rats, mice, and even other bats. Fruit bats, on the other hand, eat plant foods, such as **nectar**, fruits, leaves, and bark. After collecting food, fruit bats hang from the branch of a tree to eat it. They crush fruits between their teeth and tongue to squeeze out the juice, which they drink.

Feeding on fish

The fish-eating bat flies low over ponds and rivers to feed on fish that are swimming close to the surface of the water. Once it finds a fish, the bat flies lower still so that its hooked claws drag in the water. It then grabs the fish with its claws and bites it through the head.

The greater bulldog bat flies close to the surface of the water in its search for fish.

Vampire bats

The vampire bat is probably the most feared bat in the world because it feeds on the blood of other animals when it comes out at night. There are three types of vampire bat, and all three are found in Central and South America. The vampire bat feeds mostly on the blood of horses, pigs, and cows. It hardly ever drinks human blood.

Vampire bats can bring up food from their stomach to feed other bats in their colony.

Two small cuts

A vampire bat uses its two extra-large front teeth to make two small cuts in the skin of its prey. The bat's **saliva** contains a chemical that stops the blood of its prey from **clotting**. This makes blood flow out of the wound without stopping. During a feed, a vampire bat drinks about two tablespoons of blood.

Vampire bats do not suck blood. Instead, they sip the blood as it flows out of two tiny wounds.

Bat fact!

Although it looks nasty, a vampire bat is a fairly harmless creature and hardly ever kills its prey.

Bat flight

A bat's wings are formed from two layers of skin that are stretched over its arms and its four extra-long fingers. These powerful wings extend down both sides of its body as far as the bat's legs. A bat also has two thumbs that stick out at the top of the wings.

Wing shape

Bats with short, wide wings fly slowly and can change direction easily. This makes it easy for them to fly around trees. Bats with long, narrow wings fly quickly but cannot change direction so easily. This shape of wing is best suited for flying long distances.

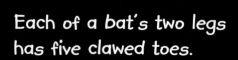

Each of a bat's two legs has five clawed toes.

Some fruit bats can hover in front of a flower to sip the nectar.

Twisting and turning

Microbats use their flying skills to hunt night-flying insects, such as moths. By changing the shape of their wings, they can twist and turn as they chase after insects. They can even swoop down and pick insects off branches or walls. Bats carry on flying while eating the insects.

Bat senses

Bats can see, hear, smell, and feel. However, hearing is their most important sense. In fact, they have the best hearing of all land mammals.

Seeing in the dark

People often say someone is 'as blind as a bat.' But bats are not blind. However, when hunting at night, hearing is much more important to a bat than seeing. As it flies around, a bat makes high-pitched sounds that humans cannot hear. These sounds bounce off objects and create echoes. The bat hears these echoes and makes a picture in its brain of where the object is and how large it is. This ability is called echolocation and is used by bats to find their way around and when hunting for food.

Bats can safely fly around obstacles in complete darkness using echolocation.

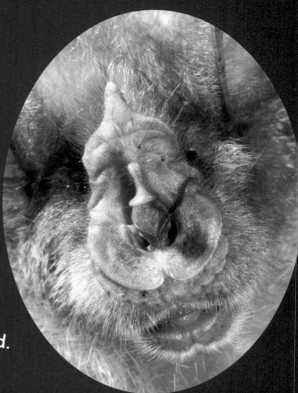

The leaf-like flap on the nose of a horseshoe bat helps it to direct sound.

Nose noises

Some bats make the sounds through their mouth. When their mouth is full of food, they cannot make sounds. Some species have solved the problem by producing sound through their nose. These bats have extra flaps on their nose, which help direct and collect sound signals.

Communication

Bats can hear the echolocation sounds made by other bats when they are hunting. However, they do not use these sounds to communicate with each other.

Instead, bats can make up to 50 different calls. Each call has its own meaning. Some calls are used when bats just want to chatter. Other sounds are made when bats want to show aggression or call their young. Male bats have special calls to attract female bats.

Vampire bats that have food to share often groom other bats first to see how full their stomach is.

These bats hanging from a cave ceiling will all have the same smell.

Spreading a scent

Bats have **scent** glands near their face and on their wings. These glands produce a special scent that bats smear over themselves and over other bats. They do this so that all bats in a colony will smell the same and can easily recognize each other.

Bat fact!

The Natterer's bat is a very talkative bat. It makes deep chirps and squeaks when it is roosting, a humming noise when it is scared, and a shrill sound when flying.

Bat helpers

Bats are very useful animals because they eat many insects that are pests. For example, bats hunt for small beetles that damage crops as well as eating lots of midges and mosquitoes.

Pollinating flowers

Bats are essential to the survival of the world's rain forest trees. When they visit flowers to drink nectar, bats pick up **pollen** and carry it to other flowers. This is called pollination. Flowers have to be pollinated before they can produce the seeds from which new plants and trees can grow.

Fruit bats roost in large trees during the day and fly in search of fruit and nectar at night.

Bat fact!

The African baobab tree relies on fruit bats to pollinate its flowers. Its flowers hang downward, open up at night, and produce nectar to attract the bats.

Spreading seeds

Fruit-eating bats also help to spread seeds around a forest. This is because the seeds inside a fruit pass through the bats' **guts** and are then released unharmed in their droppings.

Fruit bats carry fruits away from plants and help to spread the seeds.

Bats under threat

Many bats around the world are now under threat as more and more of their habitats are destroyed. Rain forests are being cut down and the grasslands on which many bats depend for their survival are being plowed to grow crops. Also, farmers are using **pesticides** to kill many of the insects that bats feed on.

Every night, millions of bats leave their cave In Thailand, many of the caves in which the wrinkle-lipped bats roost are now protected

Saving bats

Fortunately, there are now many conservation groups that are trying to protect bats. These groups are teaching people that bats are very useful creatures that eat pests, such as midges and mosquitoes, as well as helping trees to produce fruits.

Bat caves

Some bat caves are now popular with sightseers who gather at night to watch bats leave the cave to go hunting.

This small, World War Two pillbox is now a roosting place for bats.

Bat fact!

Up to a quarter of all bat species are under threat. In recent years, 12 species of bat have become extinct—they have disappeared forever.

Life cycle of a bat

Pup and mother

A female bat is ready to breed when she is two years old. After mating, she gives birth to one pup. Twins are very rare. The young bat can fly and catch its own food by the time it is about one month old. Bats live for more than 30 years in the wild. This means that, for their size, they are the longest-living mammals.

Young bat

Adult

30

Glossary

clotting when blood becomes thick and does not flow

creche a place where the young are left in care for short periods

echolocation a special ability to 'see' using sound

guts the system running through the body where food is digested

habitat the place in which an animal or plant lives

mammal an animal that gives birth to live young, rather than laying eggs. Female mammals produce milk to feed their young

Megachiroptera fruit bats, the larger of the two groups of bats, known as megabats

Microchiroptera smaller, insect-eating bats, known as microbats

nectar sugary liquid produced by flowers

pesticide a substance that is used to kill animal pests, such as aphids and blackfly

pollen the yellow dust produced by male parts of a flower

predator an animal that hunts other animals

pregnant describes a female animal that has a baby, or babies, developing inside her

roost to settle to sleep; a place where animals, such as bats, rest and sleep

saliva a watery liquid made in the mouth

scent a special smell, which can be recognized

tendon the tough connection between a muscle and a bone

tropical areas of the world close to the Equator that are warm all year around

Index